The WILDERNESS Way

SMALL GROUP STUDY
Twelve Foundational Stones for Building Unshakable Faith In a Chaotic World

Words to Thrive By

Paul Taylor and Vicki Taylor

The WILDERNESS Way

SMALL GROUP STUDY
*Twelve Foundational Stones for Building
Unshakable Faith In a Chaotic World*

With

REDEMPTION PRESS

Copyright ©2025 by Pastor Paul Taylor and Vicki Taylor. All rights reserved.

Published by Wilderness Way, www.thewildernessway.com
Distributed by Redemption Press, www.redemptionpress.com

Noncommercial interests may reproduce portions of this book without the express written permission of the author, provided the text does not exceed five hundred words. When reproducing text from this book, include the following credit line: *"The Wilderness Way*, by Pastor Paul Taylor and Vicki Taylor." Used by permission."

Commercial interests: No part of this publication may be reproduced in any form, stored in a retrieval system, or transmitted in any form by any means—electronic, photocopy, recording, or otherwise—without prior written permission of the publisher/author, except as provided by United States of America copyright law.

Unless otherwise indicated, all Scripture quotations are taken from the New King James Version. Copyright © 1982 by Thomas Nelson, Inc. Used by permission. All rights reserved.

Scripture quotations marked (NIV) are taken from the Holy Bible, New International Version®, NIV®. Copyright © 1973, 1978, 1984, 2011 by Biblica, Inc.™ Used by permission of Zondervan. All rights reserved worldwide. www.zondervan.com The "NIV" and "New International Version" are trademarks registered in the United States Patent and Trademark Office by Biblica, Inc.™

Front cover image captured by Mariola Wood.

ISBN 13: 979-8-99272-375-5

ACKNOWLEDGMENTS

All praise and glory to the real Author of
The Wilderness Way, the Lord Jesus Christ
and His blessed Holy Spirit,
who accomplishes His purpose
through ordinary men and women

Contents

Finding My Way—An Introduction	Page 1
The Cornerstone	Page 4
Stone #1: Truth	Page 8
Stone #2: Obedience	Page 16
Stone #3: Glory	Page 24
Stone #4: Love	Page 32
Stone #5: Wisdom	Page 40
Stone #6: Discernment	Page 48
Stone #7: Humility	Page 56
Stone #8: Self-Control	Page 64
Stone #9: Perseverance	Page 72
Stone #10: Forgiveness	Page 80
Stone #11: Repentance	Page 88
Stone #12: Security	Page 96
Salvation	Page 105
Closing Remarks	Page 107
Additional Resources	Page 108

INTRODUCTION

Finding My Way

FINDING MY WAY—AN INTRODUCTION

The Wilderness Way Small Group Bible Study is based on the *Wilderness Way Bible Study*, which emphasizes the importance of building a strong foundation in Christ. Salvation is a miraculous starting point, but for faith to grow and endure, believers must actively build a personal relationship with Jesus, stone by stone, rooted in God's Word. New believers risk becoming stagnant or discouraged, or drifting away without this intentional effort.

The foundation is built on the Cornerstone—Jesus Christ—and fortified with spiritual principles derived from the biblical definition of the words (or stones) outlined in the book. These foundational stones define a life of purpose, strength, and unwavering faith.

The concept of the Wilderness Way reflects the experiences of biblical figures such as Paul, Moses, and Elijah, who underwent seasons in the wilderness to prepare for their God-given missions. These examples teach us that the wilderness is not a punishment but a sacred space where God prepares His people for a greater purpose and calling.

This small group study will encourage readers to

- consider the depth of each stone for deeper transformation and intimacy with God,
- develop an unshakable foundation by studying and applying the biblical content of God's word,
- be "doers" of the Word, allowing their salvation to be active and impactful.

The goal is to grow into powerful and effective followers of Christ, deeply rooted in His truth and empowered by His Spirit.

If you are not wholly convinced that Christ is your cornerstone, please, prayerfully consider "Salvation" found on page 54.

SCRIPTURE

1 Peter 2:5—The strength of your spiritual house will always rely on the foundation you lay.

The Cornerstone

WEEK 1

WEEK 1
THE CORNERSTONE

Therefore, thus says the LORD GOD
"Behold I lay in Zion a stone for a foundation, a tried stone, a precious cornerstone,
a sure foundation; whoever believes will not act hastily"
Isaiah 28:16.

Life constantly shifts, presenting challenges and opportunities that test the stability of our faith. But our strength as Christians does not come from our efforts alone; it comes from Christ, the Cornerstone, the unchanging foundation of our faith. With Him, we are transformed—no longer outsiders but members of God's family. This foundation invites us to align every part of our lives with His **truth**.

As we surrender to God, humility becomes a powerful tool for transformation. It teaches us to release control and embrace circumstances through the lens of faith. With this perspective, we discover that **perseverance**, **forgiveness**, and **repentance** are not just lofty ideals but essential stones to our spiritual foundation.

As we come to know God through His word, a high view of God takes root. In **humility**, we allow God's **truth** to seep into our hearts, fostering **obedience**, **agape love**, **self-control**, **wisdom**, and **discernment**. When we trust that every trial is under the watchful eye of Jesus, no matter the struggle, we find **security** in Him.

Let today be a moment of reflection and recalibration. Is Christ the chief cornerstone of your life? Matthew 13:3–9 speaks of four reactions to God's word. Please be sure your faith is rooted and thriving in the cornerstone, Jesus Christ. As we seek His guidance, may we align our lives with the unshakable foundation He provides. To God be the **Glory**!

KEY MESSAGE
Life's greatest pursuit is to build a purposeful,
enduring legacy of faith on the solid Rock of Jesus Christ.

SCRIPTURE

- **Ephesians 2:19–22**—The family of God.
- **Matthew 13:3–9**—The Sower.
- **Matthew 7:24–27**—Build your life on the solid rock.

10 QUESTIONS FOR REFLECTION

1. In what ways does your life confirm that you are a child of God?

2. Are there areas where you struggle to surrender control to God?

3. What comfort and challenges do you find as a member of God's family through the church?

4. What responsibilities do you believe come with being members of God's household?

5. How did the fertile soil respond in Matthew 13:3–9?

6. What evidence is found in the parable of the Sower for the seed that found fertile ground?

7. What evidence is presented in Matthew 7:24 for the man who built his house on the rock?

8. How would you describe modern-day consequences of lives built on the sand?

9. How can a greater understanding of the twelve words presented in this study enrich your faith?

10. What steps can you take to deepen your foundation in Christ today?

CLOSING THOUGHT

Are you building your life on the solid rock of Christ or the sinking sand of worldly pursuits?

STONE #1

Truth

WEEKS 2 and 3

WEEK 2
STONE #1: TRUTH

*In the beginning was the Word,
and the Word was with God, and the Word was God.*
John 1:1

When we think about truth, we often associate it with evidence, logic, and discernment. However, the Bible declares that truth is not just a concept—it is a person. Jesus Christ boldly proclaimed, "I am the way, the truth, and the life" (John 14:6). His declaration affirms His eternal nature, self-sufficiency, and ultimate authority. Truth begins and ends with Him.

The story of Danie Jay, a woman drawn into new age practices before being led back to God's truth, illustrates the undeniable power of Jesus as the light of the world. During a shamanic ritual, a simple act of closing the blinds over a window symbolized spiritual darkness. At that moment, the scales fell from her eyes, and she recognized the darkness for what it truly was—evil. Her return to Jesus and confession of faith marked a victory of truth over deception.

This story highlights a fundamental reality: truth fiercely protects God's own. It is immovable, unchanging, and filled with grace. As believers, we are called to walk in this truth, allowing it to transform our hearts and renew our minds. Truth is not just something we understand; it's something we live.

It's fascinating to consider that there can be a difference of 1,200 miles between a compass's magnetic north and true north, the North Star. As surely as that sparkling point of light shines, giving us solid direction, Jesus is our True North, guiding us by His Holy Spirit. His word is Truth.

KEY MESSAGE

There *is* absolute truth. His name is Jesus, our True North.

SCRIPTURE

- **John 14:6**—Jesus is the way, the truth, and the life.
- **John 8:12**—Jesus is the light of the world.
- **Psalm 119:160**—God's Word is truth.

Week 2 | Truth

10 QUESTIONS FOR REFLECTION

1. What does it mean to you personally that Jesus is "the truth?"

2. How has society distorted the meaning of truth?

3. Are there areas of your life where you struggle to align with God's truth?

4. How do you discern between worldly perspectives and biblical truth?

5. How does believing in absolute truth affect your relationship with Jesus and others?

6. What does John 14:6 reveal about Jesus's role in salvation?

7. How would you describe "the light of life" in John 8:12?

8. How can you ensure that your life reflects the truth of Christ in a world filled with spiritual darkness?

9. What steps can you take to protect your heart and mind from deception?

10. How can the truth of Jesus give you confidence in times of doubt or trial?

CLOSING THOUGHT

Take time to consider these questions and scriptures. Allow God to guide your heart so that your life is more closely aligned with His absolute truth.

WEEK 3

STONE #1: TRUTH IN ACTION

I have come into the world, that I should bear witness to the truth. Everyone who is of the truth hears My voice.
John 18:37

The Bible offers an unchanging anchor in a world where truth is often subjective. Pilate's question, "What is truth?" (John 18:38), reflects the confusion that persists in our world today. But God's truth is eternal, flawless, and complete. Unlike progressive ideologies that depict God as evolving, scripture reveals His immutable nature (James 1:17).

The Bible's history, archaeology, prophecy, and eyewitness accounts confirm its authenticity and divine inspiration. For example, more than three hundred prophecies about Jesus, written centuries before His birth, were fulfilled in His life, death, and resurrection. The mathematical probability of this happening by chance is impossible, underscoring that God's truth is absolute.

As believers, we are called to reflect God's truth in our character and actions. Just as Jesus's moral compass was an extension of His truth, we are to live so that others see Him through us. Truth is not merely a belief but a foundation on which we stand, anchoring us amid life's uncertainties.

KEY MESSAGE

God is not who we think He is. He's who He says He is.

SCRIPTURE

- **John 8:31–32**—The truth will set you free.
- **James 1:17**—God does not change.
- **Ephesians 6:14**– Stand firm with the belt of truth.

Week 3 | Truth

10 QUESTIONS FOR REFLECTION

1. How does Jesus's unchanging nature provide stability in your life?

2. Why is it important to accept the Bible as absolute truth?

3. How can you share the truth of Jesus with someone who doubts or rejects it?

4. What role does prophecy play in affirming the Bible's reliability?

5. How can archaeology and history deepen your understanding of God's truth?

6. How does the fact that God's Word is flawless and unchanging affect your daily life?

7. What keeps people from exploring the truth of the Bible?

8. How does Jesus's statement in John 18:37 challenge you personally?

9. What practical steps can you take to make God's truth the foundation of your decisions?

10. How can you encourage others to explore and embrace God's truth?

CLOSING THOUGHT

Let these truths anchor your heart and guide your walk with God. God's truth is not only what we believe but what we live and share with others.

STONE #2

Obedience

WEEKS 4 and 5

WEEK 4
STONE #2: OBEDIENCE

Having confidence in your obedience,
I write you, knowing that you will do even more than I say.
Philemon 1:21

Obedience is evidence of a firm foundation in Christ. In the ultimate act of submission, Jesus stepped down from His throne to endure the cross, wearing a crown of thorns in humility and love. His obedience was not abstract; it was tangible, sacrificial, and grounded in trust in the Father. This act of surrender echoes through eternity, setting the standard for what it means to obey God.

Obedience is not optional in our journey. Scripture insists upon it. Just as God led the Israelites through the wilderness to reveal Himself and teach them obedience born of love, He invites us to trust Him in uncertain seasons. The key lies in our perspective: the more we view God as trustworthy, the more we obey Him.

Motivated by faith, ordinary individuals in the Bible achieved extraordinary outcomes through their obedience: Abel offered a worthy sacrifice, Noah built the ark, and Abraham left his home for a promised land. Their faith produced obedience, and their obedience revealed their faith. Let us follow their example, trusting that God will provide the strength and endurance to obey, even in the face of trials.

KEY MESSAGE

Obedience to God, born out of love and gratitude,
ignites God's power and purpose over our lives.

SCRIPTURE

- **Matthew 22:37–38**—Love God and others.
- **Hebrews 11:1–6**—Faith as the foundation for obedience.
- **Luke 9:23**—Denying ourselves and taking up your cross daily.

Week 4 | Obedience

10 QUESTIONS FOR REFLECTION

1. Why is love essential to obedience to God?

2. What does Jesus's obedience to the cross teach us about surrender and trust?

3. How does obedience demonstrate faith in God's promises?

4. What makes it difficult to obey God, especially in challenging circumstances?

5. How does love motivate obedience in your everyday life?

6. How has God used trials to strengthen your obedience and faith?

7. Why is obedience essential to your relationship with God?

8. How can you cultivate a heart of gratitude as a foundation for obedience?

9. What does dying to yourself and taking up your cross look like in your daily life?

10. How can reflecting on the faith of biblical heroes inspire your obedience today?

CLOSING THOUGHT

Faith produces obedience, and obedience reveals our faith. What does your obedience say about your faith?

WEEK 5
STONE #2: OBEDIENCE

*Now faith is the substance of things hoped for,
the evidence of things not seen.
Hebrews 11:1*

Obedience flows from a heart that trusts in God's promises. Faith in action defines those listed in Hebrews 11, often called the "Hall of Faith." Abel, Noah, Abraham, Moses, and many others demonstrated their faith by obeying God's commands, even when the path was unclear or the cost was high. Their lives remind us that obedience is an act of worship, flowing from a heart of gratitude for who God is and what He promises.

Yet obedience is not always easy. Jonah's story highlights the consequences of disobedience. Running from God's plan led him to despair, but even there, God's mercy met him. Similarly, the Israelites' journey through the wilderness tested their trust and obedience, but it was also an opportunity to deepen their relationship with God.

God does not call us to blind obedience but to an obedience rooted in love and faith. As we submit to Him, we are assured of His blessings, both seen and unseen. Let us lay down the burdens of self-will and follow the example of the faithful who have gone before us.

KEY MESSAGE
Obedience is faith in action.

SCRIPTURE

- **Deuteronomy 28:1–14**—Blessings of obedience.
- **Jonah 1- 3:4**—Lessons from Jonah's disobedience.
- **Matthew 7:24–27**—Building a foundation on obedience to God's word.

Week 5 | Obedience

10 QUESTIONS FOR REFLECTION

1. What do Hebrews 11 teach you about the relationship between faith and obedience?

2. How can obedience be described as an act of worship?

3. Reflecting on Jonah's story, how does disobedience impact those around you?

4. What burdens or baggage is God asking you to surrender in obedience?

5. How do the promises of blessings in Deuteronomy 28 motivate your obedience?

6. What has God revealed to you about His character through times of testing?

7. How does the Holy Spirit empower you to obey God's commands?

8. In what areas of your life is God calling you to deeper obedience today?

9. How can you find joy and purpose in obeying God's plan, even when it is uncomfortable?

10. What does Jonah's ultimate surrender teach you about God's mercy and patience?

CLOSING THOUGHT

Take time to meditate on these reflections and scriptures, allowing God to strengthen your foundation through obedience.

STONE #3

Glory

WEEKS 6 and 7

WEEK 6
STONE #3: GLORY

Jesus said to her,
"Did I not say to you that if you would believe, you would see the glory of God?"
John 11:40

God's glory is one of the Bible's most mysterious and awe-inspiring concepts. While we may grasp glimpses of its meaning through majestic landscapes, life-altering moments, or even the quiet beauty of creation, fully understanding God's glory is beyond human comprehension. His glory is infinite beauty, majesty, and perfection.

From the burning bush to the pillar of cloud and fire that guided the Israelites, God's Shekinah glory has been both a beacon of light and a tangible representation of His divine presence. Today, we experience His glory through the indwelling of the Holy Spirit, who illuminates our hearts and guides our paths.

Glory is not something we can earn or induce—it is a gift. It changes those who encounter it, just as Moses's face shone after being in God's presence. The question is not whether God's glory exists but whether we are open to seeing and reflecting it in our daily lives. The more we desire to witness and glorify God, the more He reveals Himself.

KEY MESSAGE

God's glory is the magnificence, beauty, and perfection of His character and attributes, encompassing the infinite greatness and worth of everything God is. To recognize God's glory is to see God.

SCRIPTURE

- **Exodus 33:15–18**—Moses's plea to see God's glory.
- **2 Corinthians 4:6**—God's light shining in our hearts.
- **Psalm 148:13**—His glory above earth and heaven.

10 QUESTIONS FOR REFLECTION

1. How would you define God's glory in your own words?

2. How has God revealed His glory to mankind through creation?

3. Why do you think God associates His glory with light?

4. In what ways does God's glory manifest differently in the Old Testament and New Testament?

5. How and when has God revealed His glory to you, personally? What impact did the experience have on your life?

6. What does Moses's request to see God's glory in Exodus 33 teach you about longing for God's presence?

7. How does the concept of Shekinah glory remind us of God's constant presence with His people?

8. What role does the Holy Spirit play in helping you experience God's glory today?

9. How can a deeper understanding of God's glory impact your faith and obedience?

10. How can you glorify God in your daily life?

CLOSING THOUGHT

Just as God revealed Himself to Moses to remind him that He would always go with him, He often reveals His glory to those He is preparing to serve Him.

WEEK 7
STONE #3: GLORY

Arise, shine, for your light has come!
And the glory of the Lord is risen upon you.
Isaiah 60:1

God's glory transforms everything it touches. When we encounter His glory, we become keenly aware of His infinite power and goodness, whether through creation, answered prayer, or moments of worship. His glory is a display of His majesty and an invitation to know Him deeply.

Moses's face glowed after he spent time with God because he had been in the presence of pure holiness. That same transformative power is available to us today through the Holy Spirit, who dwells within us. This is why we are to live as reflections of God's glory, not as sources of light ourselves but as mirrors that redirect His brilliance to the world.

However, reflecting God's glory requires humility. When we allow pride to creep in, we risk "touching" His glory and robbing Him of the credit due to His name. God's glory is not meant to elevate us but to leave us in humble awe with a mission to point others to Him. As we serve Him, let us remain vigilant, ensuring our hearts remain focused on His greatness and not our own accomplishments.

KEY MESSAGE

Those who live in truth and obedience will see God's glory.

SCRIPTURE

- **Exodus 34:29–35**—Moses's veiled face.
- **2 Corinthians 3:7-18**—Unveiled faces.
- **Luke 9:46–48**—The dangers of pride in ministry.

Week 7 | Glory

10 QUESTIONS FOR REFLECTION

1. What does Isaiah 60:1 teach us about the purpose of God's glory in our lives?

2. How can you become a better reflection of God's glory in your daily interactions?

3. Why did Moses wear a veil after encountering God's glory?

4. What does 2 Corinthians 3:7–18 teach us about living with unveiled faces?

5. How can pride hinder you from experiencing or reflecting God's glory?

6. How does humility play a role in glorifying God?

7. Reflect on a time when you were tempted to take credit for something God did through you. How did you handle it?

8. What safeguards can you put in place to ensure God alone receives glory in your life?

9. How do truth and obedience work in reflecting God's glory?

10. What practical steps can you take to ensure your life points others to God and not to yourself?

CLOSING THOUGHT

May these reflections deepen your understanding of God's glory and inspire you to live a life that magnifies His name.

STONE #4

Love

WEEKS 8 and 9

WEEK 8
STONE #4: LOVE

And now abide faith, hope, love, these three;
but the greatest of these is love.
1 Corinthians 13:13

Love is the key to a beautiful, fulfilling relationship with God and others. As believers, understanding the depth of God's love allows us to experience life more fully and reflect His character to the world. The Bible speaks of love in various forms: familial (storge), friendship (philos), romantic (eros), and divine (agape).

Agape love is the purest and highest form of love, rooted in God's essence. It transcends emotions and is an act of the will—a commitment to love others as God loves us. This selfless, unconditional love is most evident in Jesus's sacrifice on the cross. It empowers us to love our families more deeply, cherish our friends, and honor God in our relationships.

C. S. Lewis wisely noted that Christian love is not merely an emotion but a state of the will that seeks the best for others. This love challenges us to go beyond what is easy or comfortable to embrace the challenging yet rewarding journey of loving like Christ.

The world often distorts love, but God's Word anchors us in the truth. It reminds us that love is patient, kind, and enduring. As you meditate on God's love, consider how it transforms your relationships and strengthens your faith.

KEY MESSAGE

God's agape love transcends feelings and emotions,

challenging us to practice His unconditional love that never fails.

SCRIPTURE

- **1 John 4:8,16**—God is love.
- **Ephesians 3:17–19**—Being rooted and grounded in love.
- **Romans 8:31–39**—The inseparable love of God.

Week 8 | Love

10 QUESTIONS FOR REFLECTION

1. How does understanding the different types of love (storge, philos, eros, agape) change your perception of the word?

2. In what ways have you experienced agape love in your life?

3. Why is agape love essential to understanding God's character?

4. How does love as a "willful choice" challenge or change how you treat others?

5. Reflect on a time when you found it difficult to love someone. How can God's love guide you in such situations?

6. How do you balance the emotional and actionable aspects of love?

7. What does the command to "love your enemies" teach you about agape love?

8. Why is love foundational to the other "stones" of truth, obedience, and glory?

9. How has your understanding of love grown through your faith journey?

10. What steps can you take to better reflect God's love in your daily interactions?

CLOSING THOUGHT

Agape love is a deeper, richer love that produces enduring relationships.

WEEK 9
STONE #4: LOVE

*For God so loved the world that He gave His only begotten Son,
that whoever believes in Him should not perish but have everlasting life.*
John 3:16

God's love is extravagant, unearned, and unchanging. While human love often depends on feelings or circumstances, God's agape love is steadfast. It is not based on our worthiness but on His character.

This divine love calls us to live differently. It asks us to love those who are easy to love and those who challenge us. Jesus commanded us to love God with all our hearts and to love our neighbors as ourselves. These commands are not optional; they are the foundation of a life that honors God.

In 2 Samuel 1:17–27, we find a story that illustrates agape love perfectly. After the death of King Saul, David paid a beautiful tribute of love to him. Even though Saul had tried to kill him multiple times and caused him to live years on the run in hiding, David understood that Saul was in God's hands and vengeance was the LORD's. No wonder God called David a man after His own heart (1 Sam. 13:14).

Agape love is transformative. It enables us to forgive, to serve, and to persevere in the face of adversity. It bridges the gap between the human and the divine, showing us how to live in harmony with God and others.

When we embrace God's love, we reflect it in how we treat others. We become vessels of His grace, sharing His light in a world desperate for genuine love. As you reflect on the depth of God's love today, ask yourself how to be an instrument of His love in your community.

KEY MESSAGE

To live beyond the love of feelings and emotions to embrace God's agape love unleashes freedom and power beyond our ability to love.

SCRIPTURE

- **1 Corinthians 13:4–8**—Love's characteristics.
- **Matthew 22:37–40**—Love, the greatest commandment.
- **Colossians 3:14**—Love, the bond of perfection.

10 QUESTIONS FOR REFLECTION

1. What does John 3:16 reveal about the depth of God's love for you?

2. How does God's love differ from the world's definition of love?

3. How do the attributes of agape love outlined in 1 Corinthians 13 reflect God's love?

4. In what ways can love be an act of obedience to God?

5. How does agape love empower you to overcome bitterness or resentment?

6. What role does forgiveness play in loving others?

7. How does God's love inspire you to serve needy people?

8. Reflect on a time when you saw love in action through someone else. How did it impact you?

9. How does love bring unity within the church and community?

10. What practical steps can you take to show agape love to someone in your life today?

CLOSING THOUGHT

May these reflections deepen your understanding of God's love and inspire you to live a life that reflects His unconditional love.

STONE #5

Wisdom

WEEKS 10 and 11

WEEK 10
STONE #5: WISDOM

*The fear of the Lord is the beginning of knowledge,
but fools despise wisdom and instruction.*
Proverbs 1:7

Wisdom is not merely about gaining knowledge or life experience. True wisdom begins with reverence for the Lord, recognizing that His ways are higher than ours. King Solomon, known as the wisest man in history, explored every avenue of life—from education to indulgence—to uncover the meaning of existence. Despite his wealth, power, and unparalleled intellect, he concluded that life apart from God is meaningless.

True wisdom is a divine gift that allows us to navigate the complexities of life with discernment and purpose. It leads us to place God at the center of our thoughts and actions. Unlike earthly wisdom, which is often self-serving, godly wisdom aligns with God's will, glorifies Him, and benefits others.

When we approach God in humility, acknowledging our limitations, we open ourselves to the boundless wisdom He freely offers. In doing so, we can build lives rooted in truth, obedience, love, and God's glory. Ask yourself today: Are you seeking wisdom from the world or the Creator of all things?

KEY MESSAGE

Godly wisdom separates God's truth from what man desires to be true, leading to wise choices and abundant life.

SCRIPTURE

- **Ecclesiastes 9:13–18**—Wisdom is better than strength.
- **James 3:17**—The beauty of God's wisdom.
- **Ecclesiastes 10:10**—Wisdom brings success.

10 QUESTIONS FOR REFLECTION

What does it mean to you that "the fear of the Lord" is the beginning of wisdom?

How does the world's knowledge differ from godly wisdom?

Reflect on a time when relying on your own wisdom led to disappointment. What did you learn?

How can strength and knowledge impede gaining wisdom?

Can a man have wisdom outside of God?

According to Ecclesiastes 9:13–18, what is the value of wisdom?

How do you respond when your plans are interrupted by God's direction?

Why is humility essential when asking for wisdom?

What role does prayer play in your pursuit of wisdom?

How does God's wisdom provide peace in uncertain times?

CLOSING THOUGHT

As you can see, godly wisdom is forged through a high view of God, a commitment to His truth, and the humility to obey His commands.

Though it cost all you have, get wisdom (Proverbs 4:7).

WEEK 11
STONE #5: WISDOM

*If any of you lacks wisdom, let him ask of God,
who gives to all liberally and without reproach, and it will be given to him.*
James 1:5

Wisdom is a gift from God, available to all who humbly seek it. While worldly knowledge relies on human intellect and reasoning, godly wisdom flows from the Holy Spirit. It reveals God's will and enables us to act in ways that honor Him.

The Bible is rich with examples of individuals who sought God's wisdom and experienced extraordinary results. King Solomon asked for wisdom to lead God's people and was blessed with unparalleled understanding, wealth, and honor. However, wisdom is not a one-time request. We must continually seek it as we face new challenges and decisions.

God's wisdom guides us in ways the world cannot comprehend. It helps us prioritize eternal values over fleeting gains, make decisions rooted in love and justice, and trust God even when we do not understand His plan. Wisdom compels us to build our lives on the solid foundation of God's truth.

Today, ask God for wisdom in the specific areas where you feel uncertain. Trust that He will guide you as you step out in faith.

KEY MESSAGE

God's word, humility, and prayer
open the door to receiving God's wisdom.

SCRIPTURE

- **James 1:5–8**—Asking God for wisdom.
- **1 Corinthians 1:18–25**—God's wisdom and worldly wisdom.
- **Ephesians 5:15–17**—Walking in wisdom.

10 QUESTIONS FOR REFLECTION

1. What stipulation to receiving wisdom from God do we find in James 1:5–8?

2. How can we separate emotions and self-desires when asking God for wisdom?

3. Reflect on a time when you experienced the benefits of seeking godly wisdom.

4. What practical steps can you take to cultivate wisdom in your daily life?

5. In 1 Corinthians 1:18–25, how is worldly wisdom contrasted with God's wisdom?

6. What role does the Holy Spirit play in helping us discern wisdom?

7. What obstacles do we face today while striving to walk in God's wisdom?

8. How do faith and wisdom work together?

9. In what areas of your life are you most in need of godly wisdom?

10. How can wisdom help you grow in your relationship with God and others?

CLOSING THOUGHT

May these reflections inspire you to seek wisdom from the One who knows all things and delights in guiding His children.

STONE #6

Discernment

WEEKS 12 and 13

WEEK 12
STONE #6: DISCERNMENT

If you cry out for discernment...
then you will understand the fear of the Lord and find the knowledge of God.
Proverbs 2:3, 5

Discernment is the ability to distinguish between what is right and what is almost right. It is not just knowing right from wrong but seeing things through God's perspective. Discernment allows us to make decisions rooted in truth and guided by wisdom, love, and obedience to God's Word.

Before building a spiritual foundation on truth, my discernment was lacking. I relied on personal desires rather than seeking God's direction. But discernment is not gained overnight—it grows as we deepen our relationship with God, study His Word, and trust the Holy Spirit to guide us.

We see examples of godly discernment throughout the Bible. Abigail's quick thinking saved her family from disaster (1 Sam. 25), and Moses's life was saved due to his mother's discernment (Ex. 2). Discernment requires not only an understanding of God's ways but also the humility to apply wisdom with faith and trust in God's leading.

KEY MESSAGE

Good discernment results when you apply truth,
obedience, glory, love, and wisdom to daily decisions.

SCRIPTURE

- **Proverbs 2:10–11**—The key to discernment.
- **Philippians 1:9–11**—Love and discernment.
- **1 John 4:1**—Discerning truth from almost true.

Week 12 | Discernment

10 QUESTIONS FOR REFLECTION

1. How do you define discernment, and how does it differ from wisdom?

2. How does wisdom lead to discernment?

3. Reflect on a time when you acted on emotion rather than relying on godly discernment. What was the outcome?

4. Why is humility essential in seeking discernment?

5. According to Philippians 1:9, how do love, knowledge, and wisdom work together to provide good discernment?

6. What practices help you seek God's perspective when faced with choices?

7. How does a solid foundation in the word of God enable you to discern false teaching?

8. Why is it dangerous to rely solely on human understanding for decision-making?

9. How does discernment improve your ability to give sound advice to others?

10. What steps can you take to strengthen your discernment today?

CLOSING THOUGHT

As we cultivate the mind of Christ, good discernment becomes easier to obtain.

WEEK 13
STONE #6: DISCERNMENT

Above all else, guard your heart, for everything you do flows from it.
Proverbs 4:23 (NIV)

Discernment is critical to living a God-honoring life. It involves applying wisdom to decisions, evaluating situations through the lens of scripture, and seeking God's guidance over our desires. Without discernment, we risk being deceived by what seems right but leads us away from God's truth.

The story of the Apostle Paul and the slave girl in Acts 16 illustrates how discernment requires patience and attentiveness. Paul did not react impulsively but waited to see the girl's true spirit before acting. This deliberate approach prevented confusion and preserved the integrity of his mission.

Godly discernment also teaches us to guard our hearts, as Solomon failed to do. Though he was the wisest man on earth, his failure to apply discernment in his personal life led to poor choices with lasting consequences.

Discernment is not simply about avoiding sin but actively seeking God's best in every decision. Ask the Holy Spirit to grant you discernment in your relationships, ministry, and daily life.

KEY MESSAGE

Discernment is an ongoing pursuit rooted in a firm foundation in Christ.

SCRIPTURE

- **1 Kings 3:12, 1 Kings 11:1–4**—Solomon's poor discernment.
- **Acts 16:16–18**—Paul's discernment with the slave girl.
- **Colossians 4:2–6**—The call to prayer and discernment.

Week 13 | Discernment

10 QUESTIONS FOR REFLECTION

1. Why must good discernment always align with God's word?

2. How can discernment protect you from being deceived by appearances?

3. Reflect on a time when you waited for clarity before making a decision. What did you learn?

4. How does guarding your heart affect your ability to discern God's will?

5. Why is it important to seek God's wisdom before offering advice to others?

6. How can discernment help you identify false teachings or ungodly practices?

7. How does good discernment help you distinguish open doors to God's will … and closed doors?

8. How can discernment help you navigate difficult conversations with grace?

9. What role does prayer play in helping you develop discernment and direction from God?

10. How can you practice discernment more intentionally in your daily walk with God?

CLOSING THOUGHT

When good discernment becomes consistent, life becomes fruitful and blessed.

STONE #7

Humility

WEEKS 14 and 15

WEEK 14
STONE #7: HUMILITY

Humility and the fear of the Lord are riches of life.
Proverbs 22:4

Humility is imperative to our faith, yet it is often the most challenging to embrace. True humility requires us to see ourselves as we are—limited, flawed, and utterly dependent on God's grace—while recognizing the majesty and power of our Creator.

Humility is such a rare quality that others often mistake it for weakness, but the truth is that the humble Christian often stands on the most solid foundation, receiving his worth from a deep and abiding relationship with Christ.

Jesus modeled humility perfectly, from His birth in a stable to His ultimate sacrifice on the cross. His humility was not weakness but strength in submission to God's will. If we desire to reflect Christ in our lives, we must ask: Are we willing to embrace humility, even when it is uncomfortable?

Today, let us pray for the grace to humble ourselves before the Lord, remembering that true humility is the path to spiritual riches.

KEY MESSAGE

Humility and respect for God is the path to spiritual riches.

SCRIPTURE

- **Philippians 2:5–9**—The power of humility.
- **James 4:6, 10**—The promise of humility.
- **Proverbs 16:18**—The warning against pride.

Week 14 | Humility

10 QUESTIONS FOR REFLECTION

1. From Philippians 2:9, what was the result of Christ's humility toward His Father?

2. Reflect on a time when you were humbled by a situation. What did you learn?

3. How is humility connected to receiving God's grace?

4. Why is humility necessary to serve others effectively?

5. In what ways did Jesus demonstrate humility during His earthly ministry?

6. How does pride hinder your ability to grow spiritually?

7. How does humility lead to God's will?

8. How can humility help you navigate relationships with others?

9. What steps can you take to guard against pride in your daily walk?

10. How does humility strengthen your faith and reliance on God?

CLOSING THOUGHT

Pride rises up so naturally that it will require a constant, deliberate decision to choose humility in circumstances big and small.

WEEK 15
STONE #7: HUMILITY

When pride comes, then comes disgrace, but with the humble is wisdom.
Proverbs 11:2

The Bible consistently portrays humility as a strength, not a weakness. It is a conscious choice to place God's will above our own and to consider others before ourselves. Jesus's confrontation with the Pharisees highlights how pride can blind us to truth and cause us to resist God's work in our lives.

Humility requires action. It is seen in how we respond to correction, serve others, and submit to godly authority. Abigail's discernment and humble actions in 1 Samuel 25 are powerful examples of how humility can defuse conflict and bring peace.

When we embrace humility, we grow closer to God and become instruments of His grace to others. Like Jesus washing His disciples' feet, we are called to serve with selflessness and love, trusting that God will exalt us in His time.

> Humility is not thinking less of ourselves, but thinking of ourselves less.
> ~C. S. Lewis

KEY MESSAGE

Humility devours pride, changing one's perspective on every aspect of life.

SCRIPTURE

- **Luke 18:9–14**—Everyone who exalts himself will be humbled, and he who humbles himself will be exalted.
- **Matthew 18:1–5**—Humbling ourselves as children.
- **1 Peter 5:5–6**—The call to clothe ourselves with humility.

Week 15 | Humility

10 QUESTIONS FOR REFLECTION

1. According to Proverbs 11:2, what is the value of humility?

2. Is humility measured by your works or state of heart?

3. Reflect on a time when pride hindered your relationships. How could humility have changed the outcome?

4. Is your desire to be great or humble?

5. How does submission to godly authority demonstrate humility?

6. What does it mean to humble yourself as a child (Matthew 18:4)?

7. How can humility make you a more effective witness for Christ?

8. What does it mean to "clothe" yourself with humility?

9. In what ways does humility require courage and boldness?

10. What changes can you make to reflect more humility in your daily life?

CLOSING THOUGHT

May these reflections inspire you to embrace the power of humility in your walk with Christ.

STONE #8

Self-Control

WEEKS 16 and 17

WEEK 16
STONE #8: SELF-CONTROL

Whoever has no rule over his own spirit is like a city broken down without walls.
Proverbs 25:28

In biblical times, walls were a city's only defense against attack. Once a city's walls were breached, devastation was soon to follow. Such is the plight of those lacking self-control.

Self-control is not merely a product of willpower; it is a gift from God, cultivated through reliance on His strength. As Proverbs 29:18 states, "Where there is no revelation, the people cast off restraint; but happy is he who keeps the law."

My friend Buddy's struggle with addiction showcased the battle between self-gratification and self-control. Through prayer, accountability, and spiritual growth, Buddy experienced victory over his struggles. Although his life on earth ended before I was ready to let him go, he left a legacy of faith and humility.

Buddy was known to say, "I can't even control when I go to the bathroom. How can I believe I can control my own life?"

That statement is humble and speaks of our need to allow our self-control to come under God's control.

Buddy's life demonstrated how surrendering to God's will transforms lives and reminds us that self-control does not come from human effort alone but through surrender, discipline, and the grace of God. Through Christ, we can exchange our old nature for a new one, equipped with the power to overcome temptation.

Like a city with fortified walls, self-control protects our hearts, minds, and spirits from destructive influences, allowing our lives to glorify God.

KEY MESSAGE

Self-control allows people to live honorable lives, reflecting God's power and glory.

SCRIPTURE

- **Titus 2:11–12**—A call to righteous living.
- **1 Corinthians 9:27**—A call to practice what we preach.
- **2 Timothy 1:7**—A spirit of love, power and self-control.

Week 16 | Self-Control

10 QUESTIONS FOR REFLECTION

1. According to Titus 2:11–12, what responsibilities do we have in living a self-controlled life?

2. What role does the Holy Spirit play in self-discipline?

3. How does self-control impact our witness for Christ?

4. How can gaining self-control bring freedom from guilt and shame?

5. Reflect on a time when you exercised self-control. What was the outcome?

6. How can fear work to dismantle your self-control?

7. How can self-control positively impact your relationships with others?

8. What area of weakness will you surrender to God?

9. How does self-control bring glory to God?

10. How can building self-control strengthen your overall faith?

CLOSING THOUGHT

Self-control comes with the reputation of a steadfast Christian, earning the respect of those who need someone to help anchor their lives.

WEEK 17
STONE #8: SELF-CONTROL

I can do all things through Christ who strengthens me.
Philippians 4:13

Self-control is not merely a human attribute but a spiritual fruit cultivated by the Holy Spirit (Galatians 5:22–23). It involves walking in the Spirit, actively putting aside self-gratification for God's greater purpose.

Jesus exemplified perfect self-control while facing immense temptation in the wilderness (Matthew 4:1–11) and overwhelming anguish in Gethsemane (Matthew 26:39). By submitting His will to His Father repeatedly, His life is a blueprint for us to follow.

We must learn to yield to the Spirit and trust in God's strength to overcome the desires of the flesh. By putting on the whole armor of God (Ephesians 6:10–18), we prepare ourselves to stand firm in the face of trials and temptations.

The journey to self-control is not easy, but it is rewarding. By God's grace, we can live disciplined lives and fulfill His calling through diligence, reliance on prayer, and obedience to God's Word.

As followers of Christ, we are called to live under "new management." This transition requires relinquishing ownership of our desires and aligning our will with God's purpose. Self-control is not about perfection but persistence, rooted in daily reliance on the Holy Spirit.

KEY MESSAGE

As we pursue godly lives with all diligence, self-control is a virtue that transforms our lives.

SCRIPTURE

- **2 Peter 1:5–8**—The attributes of a foundation in Christ.
- **Galatians 5:16–22**—The battle between the Spirit and flesh.
- **1 Corinthians 10:13**—God will provide a way of escape.

Week 17 | Self-Control

10 QUESTIONS FOR REFLECTION

1. What practical steps can you take to "walk in the Spirit" daily?

2. How does self-control help you resist the temptations of the flesh?

3. How can knowing and relying on God's word arm you to resist temptation?

4. Reflect on a time when you lost self-control. How could you have responded differently?

5. What practical steps can you take to develop greater self-control?

6. How does the armor of God (Ephesians 6:10–18) empower you to live a disciplined life?

7. How does pursuing godliness work naturally to improve your self-control?

8. In what ways does self-control reflect your faith in action?

9. How does self-control help you persevere in your walk with Christ?

10. How can you encourage others to cultivate self-control in their lives?

CLOSING THOUGHT

Self-control is a daily practice that shapes us into Christ's image. Through prayer, obedience, and reliance on the Holy Spirit, we can glorify God by standing firm and steady in our faith.

WEEK 18
STONE #9: PERSEVERANCE

*And let us not grow weary while doing good,
for in due season we shall reap if we do not lose heart.*
Galatians 6:9

Faithfulness in godliness is part of perseverance, but at the heart of perseverance is the pursuit of God. We become overcomers when we keep our eyes on Him through good times and bad.

Satan would have you believe that God is not present in your trials and that you are one discouragement from falling away, but the truth is that God is ever-present in your need and doing beautiful work in you.

Romans 5:3–5 reminds us that tribulations produce perseverance, character, and hope.

Perseverance is often cultivated through trials, not in their absence. It is not about escaping difficulties but enduring them with faith, trusting that God will provide the strength to bear them.

When we cling to Jesus through our trials, perseverance produces a deeper maturity and reliance on Him.

As our foundations grow and swell through perseverance, trials no longer hold the power to strike us with fear and panic.

The Christian race isn't won by speed but by steady faithfulness. Just as the tortoise stayed the course in the classic fable, winning over the hare through perseverance, slow and steady wins the race. Those who persevere in Christ will never be put to shame.

KEY MESSAGE
God often does His best work in us
through the most challenging circumstances.

SCRIPTURE

- **James 1:2–4**—Testing of our faith produces steadfastness.
- **Hebrews 12:1–2**—Running our race with endurance.
- **2 Timothy 4:7**—Fight the good fight. Finish the race!

Week 18 | Perseverance

10 QUESTIONS FOR REFLECTION

1. How do you generally respond to trials or difficulties?

2. Why should we "count it all joy" when facing trials?

3. How have past challenges strengthened your faith and perseverance?

4. What steps can you take to stay focused on Christ when life feels overwhelming?

5. Reflect on a time when perseverance led to a significant spiritual breakthrough.

6. How does Hebrews 12:1–2 encourage you to run the race set before *you*?

7. What role does prayer play in strengthening your endurance?

8. How do we "keep the faith" even in hard times?

9. How can you encourage someone who is struggling to persevere?

10. What spiritual rewards have you experienced through perseverance?

CLOSING THOUGHT

The race is on!

Persevere for the glory of God. And then, when your race is won, join the saints in saying, "I have fought the good fight; I have finished the race; I have kept the faith."

WEEK 19
STONE #9: PERSEVERANCE

Pray without ceasing.
1 Thessalonians 4:17

Perseverance through prayer displays humility, changes lives, and draws us nearer to God. Kingston was six years old when he was diagnosed with leukemia.

As the disease ravaged his body, his doctors asked me to prepare his parents for their impending loss. As I met with them and gently began speaking, his mother, who had been praying without ceasing, looked at me with fire in her blue eyes and stated, "My son will not die. God will heal him." I believe that in her prayers, God had spoken wisdom and comfort into her heart. Kingston not only lived but is a cancer-free young man to this day.

Persistent prayer reflects a deep trust in God's ability to act in His perfect timing. When we persevere in prayer, we align ourselves with God's will, opening the door for His intervention and grace, but there is more. Persistent prayer allows us to receive God's strength and comfort when His answer is no.

There is great power to be had in persevering prayer.
~Andrew Murray

Perseverance through prayer is not demanding God do as we see fit but, by faith, submitting ourselves to His will. It transforms us, builds our character, and equips us to inspire others with God's faithfulness.

KEY MESSAGE

Persevering prayer is effective and essential in witnessing what only God can do.

Scripture

- **Romans 5:3–4**—The purpose of tribulation.
- **2 Kings 20:1–5**—God hearing and answering prayers.
- **Luke 11:9–11**—The power of persistence in prayer.

Week 19 | Perseverance

10 QUESTIONS FOR REFLECTION

1. What trials have tested your perseverance, and how did you respond?

2. How does knowing God is building your foundation through trials comfort you?

3. What role does prayer play in helping you endure life's challenges?

4. Reflect on a time when persistent prayer led to a breakthrough. What did you learn?

5. How does Hezekiah's prayer encourage you to seek God during your greatest trials?

6. What spiritual lessons can we learn from Hezekiah's account?

7. What do we learn about persistent prayer from Luke 11:9–11?

8. How does your faith in God influence your ability to endure hardships?

9. How does accepting God's response to our prayer requests testify to humility and submission to His will?

10. In what ways can you encourage others to persevere through their trials?

CLOSING THOUGHT

Sadly, Hezekiah made poor decisions during his added years and failed to finish his race well. The last stone we lay in the Wilderness Way is Security. As our foundation grows, this precious stone allows us to proclaim: My time is in God's hands. To God be the Glory.

STONE #10

Forgiveness

WEEKS 20 and 21

WEEK 20
STONE #10: FORGIVENESS

If we confess our sins, He is faithful and just to forgive us our sins and to cleanse us from all unrighteousness.
1 John 1:9

Forgiveness is a precious stone in our foundation of faith. Illustrated perfectly in the story of the prodigal son (Luke 15:11–24), we see our Father's compassion, unconditional love, and eagerness to forgive. The youngest son's journey represents humanity's tendency to stray from God, seeking fulfillment in worldly pursuits. Yet the father's response—running to meet his son with open arms—is a vivid reminder of God's overwhelming mercy and love.

The prodigal's decision to leave home was rooted in pride and a desire for independence. But hardship humbled him, driving him back to his father in repentance. Despite the older brother's bitterness, the father's joy at his son's return reveals the boundless nature of true forgiveness.

God's forgiveness is not based on our merit but on His grace. If you find yourself distant from God, remember that He is watching, ready to welcome you home with celebration. Forgiveness is a divine gift, and its power to restore relationships and peace is unparalleled.

KEY MESSAGE
Humility and repentance hold the keys to our Father's house.

SCRIPTURE
- **Luke 15:11–24**—The biblical account of the prodigal son.
- **Psalm 103:12**—The completeness of God's forgiveness.
- **Ephesians 4:32**—Being kind and forgiving as Christ forgave you.

Week 20 | Forgiveness

10 QUESTIONS FOR REFLECTION

1. What emotions might the father have experienced as his youngest son left home?

2. What role did the son's suffering play in leading him back to his father?

3. How did the father demonstrate forgiveness and unconditional love?

4. What lessons can we learn from the older brother's reaction to the celebration?

5. How does this parable mirror our relationship with God?

6. Have you ever experienced a time when you needed to return to God in repentance? What choice did you make?

7. Why do you think the father didn't go after his son?

8. What barriers keep people from seeking God's forgiveness?

9. How can we reflect the Father's forgiveness in our own relationships?

10. What does the Father's joy teach us about God's heart for those who lose their way?

CLOSING THOUGHT

No matter how far we wander into the wilderness, we can always journey back to the peace and safety of our Father's house.

WEEK 21
STONE #10: FORGIVENESS

For all have sinned and fall short of the glory of God.
Romans 3:23

Forgiveness is not merely an act of mercy; it is an act of freedom. Whether we forgive others, seek forgiveness, or forgive ourselves, it releases us from bitterness, guilt, and shame. Without forgiveness, we remain shackled by the wounds of the past, unable to move forward in God's peace.

The fall of Adam and Eve (Genesis 3) demonstrates humanity's tendency to sin and blame others, yet God's response included forgiveness and grace. Similarly, Jesus's sacrifice on the cross provided the ultimate act of forgiveness, extending mercy to all who seek it.

Forgiveness also involves humility. Releasing grudges and forgiving ourselves requires surrendering pride and embracing God's truth about who we are—redeemed and loved. Without understanding our sinful nature and the price Jesus paid for forgiveness, we will find it difficult to forgive others, but as our foundation grows, so will our ability to "Let it Go."

> Forgiveness unleashes joy. It brings peace. It washes the slate clean.
> It sets all the highest values of love in motion.
> ~George MacDonald

When we forgive, we reflect God's character, bringing healing and reconciliation to our relationships.

KEY MESSAGE

Unforgiveness is too costly to hang on to. Let it go!

SCRIPTURE

- **Romans 5:8**—Christ died for us while we were still sinners.
- **Matthew 18:21–35**—Forgiving as you have been forgiven.
- **Colossians 3:12–15**—Putting on the attributes of Christ.

10 QUESTIONS FOR REFLECTION

1. Why is forgiveness essential to a healthy spiritual life?

2. How does unforgiveness affect your relationship with God and others?

3. What does the parable of the unforgiving servant teach us about forgiveness?

4. How does God's forgiveness inspire us to forgive others?

5. Why is self-forgiveness often harder than forgiving others?

6. Have you experienced healing through forgiving someone?

7. How does forgiveness free you from the burdens of guilt and bitterness?

8. Why is love the key to forgiveness, as described in Colossians 3:14?

9. Who is it time for you to forgive today?

10. How does the act of forgiving reflect spiritual growth?

CLOSING THOUGHT

Forgiveness is one of the most powerful gifts we can give and receive. It restores what is broken, reflects God's character, and brings freedom to our hearts. Whether forgiving others, seeking forgiveness, or forgiving yourself, take the step today to release the past and embrace God's freedom to move forward unhindered.

STONE #11

Repentance

WEEKS 22 and 23

WEEK 22
STONE #11: REPENTANCE

Bear fruit in keeping with repentance.
Matthew 3:8

Repentance is not a mere acknowledgment of wrongdoing but an invitation to restoration. It is the act of turning away from sin and toward God, embracing His mercy and grace. Repentance begins with humility, continues through conviction, and culminates in transformation. It is the first step of our faith journey and a practice that deepens as we grow closer to Christ.

In Psalm 51:3, David expresses the weight of his sin, recognizing it as ever-present. His honesty and willingness to confront his guilt remind us of the power of repentance to restore fellowship with God. True repentance isn't about perfection but a posture of the heart that seeks to align with God's will.

Repentance is ongoing because our sinful nature is persistent. Yet God's grace is sufficient to cover every transgression. As we turn to Him in repentance, we experience His cleansing power, a renewed mind, and the strength to walk in righteousness.

KEY MESSAGE

True repentance restores our relationship with God, broken by sin.

SCRIPTURE

- **Psalm 51:3–12**—David's prayer of repentance.
- **Acts 3:19**—Repent and be refreshed by the Lord.
- **Proverbs 28:13**—Transparency with God.

Week 22 | Repentance

10 QUESTIONS FOR REFLECTION

1. Why is repentance essential to our relationship with God?

2. What is the difference between remorse and repentance?

3. How does repentance transform us into the "new man" described in Ephesians 4:24?

4. Why is it important to not only confess our sins but also turn away from them?

5. How does repentance reflect humility in our walk with Christ?

6. What role does the Holy Spirit play in convicting us of sin?

7. How has repentance brought renewal to your life in the past?

8. Why does God call us to ongoing repentance, even after we are saved?

9. How does repentance lead to deeper worship and gratitude toward God?

10. How can you practice repentance daily in your spiritual walk?

CLOSING THOUGHT

It is impossible to hide our sins from God, but His grace invites us to repentance, refreshment, and new beginnings.

WEEK 23
STONE #11: REPENTANCE

*I say to you,
there is joy in the presence of the angels of God over one sinner who repents.*
Luke 15:10

Repentance extends beyond our relationship with God to include earning the trust and respect of others. From the moment of our repentance that led to salvation, we can show the power of repentance to change lives. It demonstrates humility, fosters healing, and reflects God's grace to those around us.

In Acts 9, Saul (Paul) encounters God on his way to Damascus to persecute Christians. Even though his encounter is so profound that it changes his heart completely, others are not immediately convinced of his sincere repentance. However, as Paul persevered, he became the apostle to the Gentiles and the author of thirteen books in the Bible.

True repentance requires regular, prayerful self-examination. Let Psalm 139:23 become our humble plea to God. When we allow the Holy Spirit to search our hearts, we become more aware of the areas where we need transformation. Repentance is a gift that leads us to freedom, peace, and closer fellowship with God.

KEY MESSAGE

The evidence of true repentance is a changed life.

SCRIPTURE

- **Acts 9:1–19**—From an enemy of God to a servant.
- **Romans 2:4**—God's kindness leads us to repentance.
- **1 John 1:8–9**—If we confess our sins, He is faithful to forgive.

Week 23 | Repentance

10 QUESTIONS FOR REFLECTION

1. When has God's Spirit led you to repentance? ? In what ways did you change through the experience?

2. What response have you received from others who have learned of your repentance?

3. How can you show humility and patience toward those who doubt your sincerity?

4. What lessons can we learn from Ananias's response to God's command to go to Saul?

5. Have you ever experienced the freedom that comes from asking forgiveness from someone you wronged?

6. What prevents us from approaching others to ask for forgiveness?

7. How can repentance strengthen broken relationships?

8. How does repentance help us become more Christlike?

9. Is repentance a frequent occurrence in your life?

10. How does repentance lead to greater intimacy with God?

CLOSING THOUGHT

Repentance is not a one-and-done action but a lifelong journey of asking God's forgiveness as we become aware of our sins. It is both an acknowledgment of our need for His grace and an active decision to pursue righteousness. Through repentance, we are steadily transformed into the image of Christ, empowered to walk in freedom and faith.

STONE #12

Security

WEEKS 24 and 25

WEEK 24
STONE #12: SECURITY

*All that the Father gives Me will come to Me,
and the one who comes to Me I will by no means cast out.*
John 6:37

The world offers many substitutes for security—wealth, status, relationships, or achievements—but none can provide the lasting peace and safety we find in Christ. In Romans 8:31, Paul boldly declares, "If God is for us, who can be against us?" This simple yet profound truth reminds us that God's unwavering presence is our ultimate assurance.

John 5:24 assures believers that their escape from God's judgment and transformation from life to death are not future events but occur the moment they surrender their hearts and lives to Jesus.

Unfailing security stems from God's unshakable promises. Through His Word, we see that His love, forgiveness, and faithfulness never waver. He remains the same yesterday, today, and forever. Our salvation is not dependent on our works or feelings but on His grace. As believers, we are held securely in His hands, and no spiritual or physical force can remove us.

This security is not just about eternity; it impacts our daily lives. When we understand that our identity and worth are secure in Christ, we can step out in faith, boldly proclaim the gospel, and trust God through every trial.

KEY MESSAGE

If Christ is your Savior, your future here and in heaven is secure.

SCRIPTURE

- **John 5:24**— Believers have crossed from death to life.
- **Psalm 4:8**—God alone provides peace and safety.
- **John 10:27–29**—Jesus holds us securely in His hands.

10 QUESTIONS FOR REFLECTION

1. How does knowing you are held secure in God's hands impact how you process life?

2. What worldly things have you sought for security in the past, and how do they compare to Christ's promises?

3. How can you strengthen your confidence in God's promises?

4. How does Romans 8:31 encourage you?

5. How does knowing God is unchanging affect your thoughts on security?

6. How can reflecting on your salvation deepen your sense of security in Christ?

7. Why is it important to remember that God's security does not eliminate challenges but provides peace amid them?

8. How important is trusting God when the future is uncertain?

9. How has God proven His faithfulness to you in times of doubt or fear?

10. How can you encourage others to find security in Christ?

CLOSING THOUGHT

The phrase "Do not fear, or do not be afraid" appears 365 times in the Bible, one for every day of the year. From Truth to Security, the key to living fearlessly is building an unshakable foundation in Christ.

WEEK 25
STONE #12–SECURITY

*Let us hold fast the confession of our hope without wavering,
for He who promised is faithful.*
Hebrews 10:23

God's faithfulness to His people is a recurring theme throughout the Bible. Despite Israel's rebellion, doubts, and failures, God never abandoned them. He guided them through the wilderness, provided for their needs, and brought them to the promised land. Similarly, God's love for us is steadfast, even when we falter.

The twelve stones in Joshua 4 were a tangible reminder of God's miraculous power and faithfulness in leading Israel across the Jordan River on dry ground. Just as the Israelites laid down those stones as a memorial, we can lay spiritual markers of faith throughout our lives. These markers remind us that God's promises are unchanging, His love is unwavering, and His presence is constant. He is faithful.

When we reflect on what God has done for us, we find the strength to face future challenges confidently. We can rest secure in His promises, knowing He is always with us and for us.

KEY MESSAGE

God is unwaveringly faithful to His word.
What He said He will do, He will do.

SCRIPTURE

- **Joshua 4:1–7**—Twelve memorial stones God's faithfulness.
- **Isaiah 54:10**—God's unshakable kindness and mercy.
- **Psalm 111:2–4** –Remembering God's works.

Week 25 | Security

10 QUESTIONS FOR REFLECTION

1. Why did God instruct the Israelites to erect a memorial?

2. How does remembering God's past provisions help you trust Him in the present?

3. What life experiences have served as markers of God's faithfulness?

4. What areas of your life do you need to surrender to God?

5. How does God's faithfulness to Israel encourage you in your walk of faith?

6. What steps can you take to build your trust in God's promises?

7. How does reflecting on your identity in Christ strengthen your sense of security?

8. How can you share the message of God's faithfulness with others?

9. How can building a deeper foundation free you from fear and anxiety?

10. How can you use the twelve stones of the Wilderness Way to build your memorial of God's faithfulness?

CLOSING THOUGHT

Our security in Christ is found in the culmination of every foundational stone: truth, obedience, love, wisdom, and more. Each stone strengthens our confidence in God's unwavering presence and eternal promises.

Salvation

SALVATION

Salvation is not about a specific prayer or an emotional experience; it's about surrendering our hearts and lives to Jesus Christ as Lord and Savior, allowing Him to transform our lives into His likeness. It begins with acknowledging that Jesus is "the way, the truth, and the life" (John 14:6) and continues with a lifelong commitment to following Him. Salvation rests entirely on the work of Christ and the grace of God, not on human effort.

KEY ELEMENTS OF SALVATION INCLUDE THE FOLLOWING:

1. **Faith in Jesus Christ**—Trusting Him as the Son of God and Savior.
2. **Repentance**—Turning away from sin and seeking to live according to His word.
3. **Adoption into God's Family**—Believers are welcomed into God's spiritual family and joyfully assume the responsibilities of becoming a part of the body of Christ.
4. **Freedom and Security in Christ**—Through salvation, believers are no longer bound by sin and are assured of their eternal destiny with God.

SCRIPTURE

- **Romans 10:9-10**—"If you confess with your mouth the Lord Jesus and believe in your heart that God has raised Him from the dead, you will be saved."
- **John 14:6**—"I am the way, the truth, and the life. No one comes to the Father except through Me."
- **2 Corinthians 5:17**—"Therefore, if anyone is in Christ, he is a new creation; old things have passed away; behold, all things have become new."
- **John 1:12**—"But as many as received Him, to them He gave the right to become children of God."
- **John 10:28**—"And I give them eternal life, and they shall never perish; neither shall anyone snatch them out of My hand."

CLOSING REMARKS

If you have come to Christ through this study,
PRAISE the LORD! We would love to celebrate with you.
Please share your story with us at wildernesswaystudy@gmail.com.
May God bless your journey of faith!

ADDITIONAL RESOURCES

As this small group study draws to a close, I pray these twelve stones have found a place in your foundation of faith. As you move forward in your faith journey, I encourage you to take the Wilderness Way with you. Dig deeper into the depth of these stones through the following:

- The Wilderness Way Bible Study: Twelve Foundational Stones for Building Unshakable Faith in a Chaotic World.
- The Wilderness Way 55+ Remembering the Faithfulness of Jesus: A Guided Journal
- The Wilderness Way for Kids Leader's Guide: An Interactive Bible Study for Children to Learn the Same Twelve Stones Presented in the Adult Study
- Please consider journalling the Wilderness Way. Set up your journal using the twelve stones of Truth, Obedience, Glory, etc., and record the struggles and lessons that God is teaching you throughout your pilgrimage of faith.

Please visit our website at thewildernessway.com to learn more and discover what's new in the Wilderness Way.

We'd love to hear your testimony if God has used The Wilderness Way to enrich your faith. Please email us at wildernesswaystudy@gmail.com

God bless you for studying the Wilderness Way! I hope you have discovered that these truly are Words to Thrive By!

ORDER INFORMATION

To order individual copies go to
redemption-press.com/bookstore

For discounts on bulk orders
send an email to
bookorders@redemption-press.com.
subject: bulk orders

www.ingramcontent.com/pod-product-compliance
Lightning Source LLC
Chambersburg PA
CBHW022115090426
42743CB00008B/855